weblinks

You don't need a computer to use this book. But, for readers who do have access to the Internet, the book provides links to recommended websites which offer additional information and resources on the subject.

You will find weblinks boxes like this on some pages of the book.

weblinks

For more information about a specific topic here, go to www.waylinks.co.uk/series/religiontoday/Judaism

waylinks.co.uk

To help you find the recommended websites easily and quickly, weblinks are provided on our own website, **waylinks.co.uk.** These take you straight to the relevant websites and save you typing in the Internet address yourself.

Internet safety

↗ Never give out personal details, which include: your name, address, school, telephone number, email address, password and mobile number.

↗ Do not respond to messages which make you feel uncomfortable – tell an adult.

↗ Do not arrange to meet in person someone you have met on the Internet.

↗ Never send your picture or anything else to an online friend without a parent's or teacher's permission.

↗ If you see anything that worries you, tell an adult.

A note to adults
Internet use by children should be supervised. We recommend that you install filtering software which blocks unsuitable material.

Website content

The weblinks for this book are checked and updated regularly. However, because of the nature of the Internet, the content of a website may change at any time, or a website may close down without notice. While the Publishers regret any inconvenience this may cause readers, they cannot be responsible for the content of any website other than their own.

Judaism

Gianna Quaglia

WAYLAND

First published in 2007 by Wayland

This book is based on *21st Century Judaism* by Michael Keene
originally published by Wayland.

Wayland
338 Euston Road
London NW1 3BH

Wayland Australia
Hachette Children's Books
Level 17 207 Kent Street
Sydney, NSW 2000

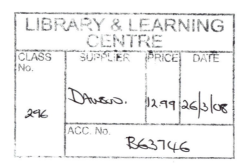

Produced for Wayland by Discovery Books

Maps and artwork: Peter Bull

British Library Cataloguing in Publication Data
Quaglia, Gianna
   Judaism. - (World religions today)
   1. Judaism - Juvenile literature
   I. Title
   296

 ISBN-13: 978 07502 5264 5

Printed in China

Wayland is a division of Hachette Children's Books,
an Hachette Livre UK company

The publisher would like to thank the following for permission
to reproduce their pictures: PNC/Brand X/Corbis cover;
Art Directors/I. Genut 24; Bridgeman Art Library
www.bridgeman.co.uk/West London Synagogue, UK 10,
Palazzo Ducale, Urbino, Italy 13, Stapleton Collection, UK 14,
Private Collection 25; CIRCA Photo Library/ Barrie Searle 18,
19, 26, 29; Corbis/David Rubinger 9, Hanan Isachar 39,
Alexander Demianchuk/Reuters 43, Reuters 45; Eye
Ubiquitous 7; Jewish Museum, Berlin/Jens Ziehe 41; Robert
Harding Picture Library/S. Grandadam 15, ASAP 21, A.
Simmenauer 33, Photri 35; Hutchison Picture Library 5; Alex
Keene 23; Ann and Bury Peerless 8, 20; Zev Radovan 28, 36,
44; Topfoto 4, 16, 17, 22, 27, 30, 31, 32, 34, 37, 38, 42

Contents

Note

In the Western world, years are numbered as either BC ('Before Christ') or AD (Anno Domini – which is Latin for 'In the year of our Lord…'). In this book, the more neutral terms BCE ('Before the Common Era') and CE ('Common Era') are used. The Jewish calendar gives the year of creation as 3760BCE. This means that the year 2000CE was 5760-5761 in the Jewish calendar.

Introduction

Judaism goes back thousands of years. Jews have a strong sense of community. It is like belonging to a special family. For many Jews, being Jewish means sharing a common history with others.

The Jewish 'family'

Judaism is one of the oldest religions in the world. It began over three thousand years ago. Today there are just over 13 million Jews in the world. Judaism is like one, very large 'family'. Belonging to this Jewish 'family' means accepting a whole way of life.

Just like any large family, the Jewish family is made up of people with very different opinions, who like to live and worship in different ways. Some Jews, called '**secular** Jews', do not live a religious life, but they may still feel that they are a part of the Jewish community.

Jews come from Israel, in the Middle East. At first they were called '**Israelites**'. They have their own language, called Hebrew. The word 'Jew' comes from 'Judah', the name of one of the tribes that lived in Israel.

◄ *A Jewish boy lights a special candlestick during Hanukkah (see page 34).*

In our own words

"All Jews are part of a long, and very proud, religious tradition. We feel a link with all the Jews who have lived and suffered, back to the time of our father, Abraham. There is no single Jewish way that we all follow. Judaism is like a 'family'. We sometimes argue with other members of the 'family' and fall out, but we usually make up. I have never met anyone who was not, deep down, proud to be a Jew."

Deborah, aged 16, UK

▲ A father and son sit together during worship in a synagogue in London, UK. The father is wearing his tallit (prayer shawl), as he does every time he prays in the **synagogue** (see page 30), and his son has a kippah (skullcap) on his head.

Where do Jews live?

Throughout history, Jews have always had to move around. They were often **persecuted** and forced to leave their homes. Because of this, there are Jews all over the world.

Two traditions

There are two main Jewish traditions – the Ashkenazim and the Sephardim. The Ashkenazim are Jews that first lived in France and Germany. They then moved to central and Eastern Europe. They had their own culture and their own language – Yiddish, a mixture of German and Hebrew. Today, most of the Jews living in the United States are descendants of the Ashkenazim tradition. Many others live in Israel and Australia.

Sephardim are Jews who first lived in Spain and Portugal. In 1492 the Christian rulers of Spain forced them to leave. These Jews settled in North Africa, Greece, Italy and the **Ottoman Empire**. The Sephardim also had their own culture and their own language – Ladino, a mixture of Spanish and Hebrew.

▼ *This map shows where Jews live today.*

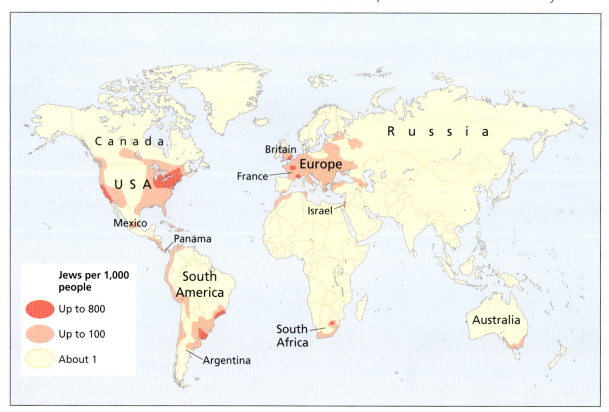

Jews per 1,000 people

- Up to 800
- Up to 100
- About 1

The spread of the Jews

Many Jews live in the USA. There are 5.5 million American Jews. Almost one million Jews live in New York.

There are about 6 million Jews living in Israel. There has always been a small Jewish community in Israel. But many European Jews started to move to Israel in the late 19th and early 20th centuries. More Jews arrived after the Second World War (1939-45). When the state of Israel was founded (1948), Jews arrived from all over the world, including Iran and Iraq, Ethiopia and Yemen. Almost 300,000 Jews now live in Great Britain. Almost all of them live in London and the southeast of England.

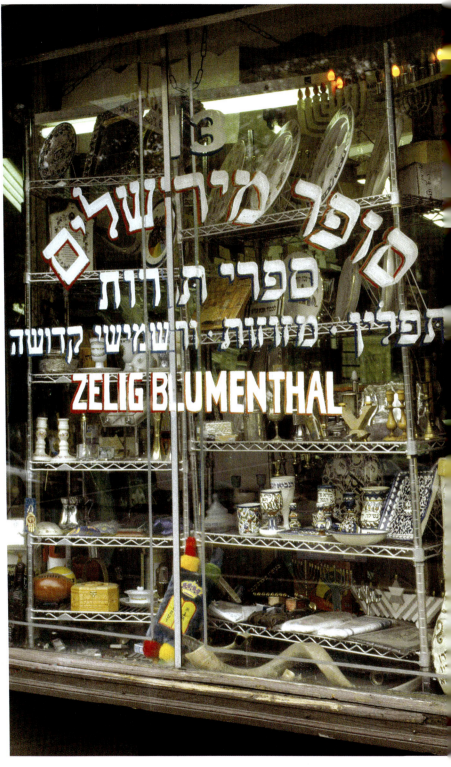

▲ *A shop front in a Jewish area of New York City, USA. The city of New York has more Jews than any other city in the world.*

Jewish groups

There are four main Jewish groups: **Orthodox** Jews and three groups of **Progressive** Jews: Masorti, Reform and Liberal Jews. Masorti Jews are also known as Conservative Jews.

Orthodox Jews

Most Jews in Great Britain and in Israel are members of an Orthodox synagogue. But in the USA, only ten per cent of the Jews who live there are Orthodox. Orthodox Jews believe that the **Torah**, the first five books of the Bible, is God's eternal word and can never change. In an Orthodox synagogue men and women sit separately, and the Hebrew language is used in all services. Women do not lead services in the synagogue. The **Sabbath** day is strictly a day of rest, and there are special rules about food.

Progressive Jews

There are many kinds of Progressive Jews, including Reform and Liberal

▲ *A Jewish boy walks along a street in Jerusalem carrying a Torah scroll. It is the boy's Bar Mitzvah (see page 37).*

(see page 37)

Jews. Both Reform and Liberal Jews believe that certain aspects of Judaism should change with the times. Men and women sit together in Progressive synagogues, and services are held in the everyday language of worshippers. Women are allowed to be **rabbis**.

Masorti Jews

Masorti, or Conservative, Jews are traditional Jews who believe that

➤ *Rabbi Naamah Kelman was the first female rabbi in Israel. While services in an Orthodox synagogue can only be taken by a male rabbi, women can be rabbis in other synagogues.*

Judaism has changed over the centuries and will continue to change in the future. Each individual synagogue can decide how traditional its services should be.

Ten basic facts about Judaism

1 Judaism began more than 3,000 years ago.
2 Jews worship one God.
3 There are about 13 million Jews in the world today.
4 A Jewish place of worship is called a synagogue.
5 The Torah is the first five books of the Bible.
6 The scrolls of the Torah sit in the **Ark** – a cupboard at the front of the synagogue.
7 The best-known Jewish symbols are the six-pointed Star of David and the seven-branched candlestick (the *menorah*).
8 Jews trace their ancestry back to Abraham, the father of their nation, and to Moses, who gave them the Torah.
9 The Sabbath day (*Shabbat*) is a day of rest for all Jews. It starts about half an hour before the beginning of sunset every Friday and ends when the stars appear in the sky on Saturday night.
10 Jews have their own calendar. This calendar is 3,761 years ahead of the Western calendar.

1 History of the Jews

Judaism began with Abraham, who lived nearly four thousand years ago in about 1800BCE. Some Jews believe that Abraham is the founder of the Jewish people.

Abraham

Abraham was brought up in the small town of Ur, in modern-day Iraq. His family worshipped many gods. But Abraham began to believe in one God who created the world and who watched over people. God made a promise to Abraham. God promised him that his followers and descendants would be God's 'Chosen people'. They would be different from other people because of their special relationship with God.

➤ *This modern painting shows Abraham about to offer his son, Isaac, as a sacrifice to God. Jews believe that this was a test of Abraham's faith in God.*

10

Founding fathers

God told Abraham to take his family to a new country, Canaan, now called Israel. God also promised that Abraham's descendants would become a great nation. Even though Abraham's wife, Sarah, was old, she gave birth to a son called Isaac. Some Jews believe that they are descendants of Abraham and that he is the founding father of their religion. Abraham's son, Isaac, and his grandson, Jacob, are also founding fathers.

God's promise to Abraham

According to the Torah, the holy book of the Jews, this is God's promise to Abraham:

'*I will make you a great nation and I will bless you;
I will make your name great, and you will be a blessing.
I will bless those who bless you, and whoever curses you I will curse and all peoples on earth will be blessed through you.*'

(Genesis 12:2-3)

▼ *This map shows the route taken by Abraham when he and his family moved.*

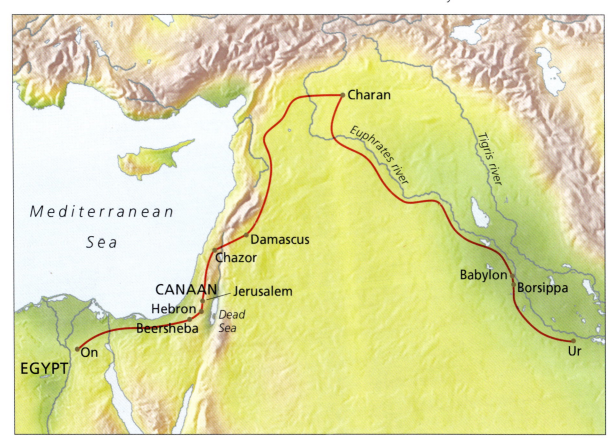

Moses

The greatest of all the Jewish **prophets** was Moses. He lived about 600 years after Abraham.

The Israelites in Egypt

At this time, Jews were called 'Israelites' after their ancestor Jacob, who was also called 'Israel'. In about 1650BCE, the Israelites went to Egypt to find food after a **famine** in Canaan. But the Egyptian king, or Pharaoh, treated them very badly, and forced them to work as slaves. By the time of Moses, the Israelites had been slaves in Egypt for over 400 years.

Moses told the Pharaoh that many disasters would happen if he did not release the Israelites. When the Pharaoh refused, ten terrible **plagues** hit Egypt. After the last one, the Pharaoh released the Israelites.

It took the Israelites forty years to travel back to Canaan (Israel). On this journey, known as the Exodus, Moses was given some laws from God on Mount Sinai. The most important of these laws are called the Ten Commandments.

▼ *This map shows the route taken by the Israelites when they left Egypt and travelled to Canaan. The journey took them 40 years.*

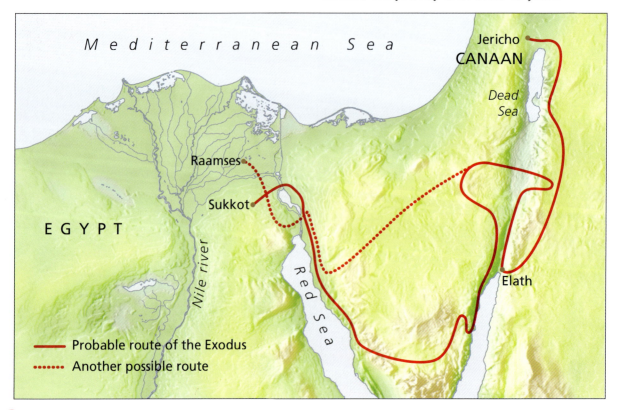

The Ten Commandments

The Ten Commandments are the basis of the Jewish faith. They also contain laws that are followed by people in most societies. They are:

1 *I am the Lord your God. You must obey no other gods but me*

2 *You must not make any **idols** to worship*

3 *You must not use God's name when swearing*

4 *You must remember to keep the Sabbath day holy*

5 *You must respect your mother and father and obey them*

6 *You must not kill*

7 *You must not commit **adultery***

8 *You must not steal*

9 *You must not tell lies or spread rumours about other people*

10 *You must not covet (want something that does not belong to you)*

▼ In this painting, Moses reveals the Ten Commandments. The Ten Commandments were written in Hebrew on stone tablets.

Wars and exile

In Canaan, the Jews had many kings, starting with Saul. He was followed by David and Solomon, David's son. Solomon was famous for his wisdom. He built a great **Temple** in Jerusalem. After Solomon died, Canaan was divided into two parts, Israel and Judah. The people who lived in Judah became known as Jews. In 772BCE, Israel was invaded by the **Assyrians**. In 586BCE, Judah was invaded by the **Babylonians**.

The old Temple was destroyed and the Jews were **exiled**. The communities of Jews that settled outside Israel were later known as the *Diaspora*.

Over the centuries, Jews began to return to their homeland. Then in 63BCE Judah was invaded by the Romans. At first the Romans let the Jews practise their religion. But in 70CE they destroyed the rebuilt

▼ *This 15th-century sketch shows Jerusalem with the Temple of Solomon at its centre.*

Temple and stopped the Jews from living in – or even entering – Jerusalem. They also outlawed Jewish education and killed any Jews who taught their young. Most of the Jews had to leave.

New lands

After that, groups of Jews settled in many different countries. The Jews had only two things left – their God and their traditions. But still they were not trusted by their new neighbours in many countries. Christian countries were often the worst places for Jews to live. Jews were persecuted in many ways. Their property was taken away, they were thrown out of the country and sometimes they were killed. Jews were thrown out of England in 1290, for example, from parts of France in 1306 and from Spain in 1492. The Jews that tried to stay in Spain were often caught and tried by a special court called the **Inquisition**. These courts used torture and death to persuade Jews to **convert**.

In the 19th century Russian Jewish families were often forced to leave their homes. They had to settle in dangerous parts of the country. But the worst persecution was the **Holocaust**, in the 20th century.

weblinks

-For more information about the Western Wall go to: www.waylinks.co.uk/series/religiontoday/Judaism

The Temple of Solomon

The Temple that Solomon built in Jerusalem was magnificent. About 180,000 people helped build it. It was the place where three important Jewish festivals – Pesach, Sukkot *and* Shavuot *– were celebrated. It was destroyed in* 586BCE *although a much larger Temple, built by Herod the Great, replaced it. Then that, too, was destroyed in* 70CE *by the Romans. The Temple has never been rebuilt.*

▲ *The only wall of Herod's Temple in Jerusalem that still exists is one of the holiest sites in Judaism. It is known as the Western Wall.*

The Holocaust

In Germany, in the 1930s, Jews once more faced persecution and danger. The leader of Germany, Adolf Hitler, hated the Jews and blamed them for every problem faced by his country.

Hitler had a plan to destroy the Jews completely. It began during the Second World War (1939-45). Hitler called this plan 'The Final Solution'. At first, all Jews had to register at a local office and wear a yellow Star of David on their clothes. Later their businesses were destroyed, their children were not allowed to go to school and Jews could not own cars. Jews were forced to move into ghettos, walled-in areas of towns and cities, where they lived in overcrowded conditions, with little food. Finally, Jews were rounded up and sent to **concentration camps**. Six million Jews, including one million children, were killed. This time of horrific persecution and death is known as the Holocaust – 'a time of raging fire'.

▼ *Jews in Warsaw, Poland, surrender to German soldiers in 1943.*

The State of Israel

During the 19th century, a group of Jews called Zionists called out for a separate Jewish state to be set up in Palestine, the area where Jerusalem is. On 14 May 1948 Palestine was divided up and the modern state of Israel was formed. Jews from all over the world began to travel to this new country to make their home there.

When Israel was created, fighting began between Jewish Israelis and

▲ An Israeli soldier arrests a Palestinian. Israelis and Palestinians have continued to fight each other since 1948.

weblinks

For more information about the Holocaust, go to:
www.waylinks.co.uk/series/religiontoday/Judaism

non-Jewish Palestinians. But the Israelis would not give up any of the land that they believed God had given them thousands of years ago. Today, many people are still trying to make peace in the state of Israel.

2 Beliefs and holy books

Jews believe in one, invisible, eternal God. They also believe that they have a special relationship with God. Jews believe that life in this world is very precious. They also believe that there is a life after death.

God

The first Hebrew that most Jewish children learn is a prayer called the **Shema**. The words of the Shema are taken from the **Scriptures**. The Shema says that there is only one God who created the world.

Religious Jews repeat the Shema twice each day – first thing in the morning and last thing at night.

▼ *A Jewish woman shields her eyes as she prays. This is to show respect for God.*

The Covenant

Jews have always believed that they have a special relationship with God. According to Jewish Scriptures this relationship is built on a covenant, or agreement, which was made between God and Abraham thousands of years ago. God promised to give the Israelites a country of their own. In return God told the Israelites to worship him only.

The Jews are sometimes known as 'Chosen People'. This means that Jews have been called by God to fulfil his commandments and to be a blessing to the world.

How the Shema begins

'Hear, O Israel, the Lord is our God. You shall love the Lord your God with all your heart, with all your soul and with all your mind. These words which I command you this day you shall take to heart. You shall teach them diligently to your children. You shall recite them when you are at home and when you are away, morning and night. You shall bind them as a sign on your hand, they shall be a reminder above your eyes and you shall inscribe them on the doorposts of your home and on your gates.'

weblinks▸

For an explanation of Jewish beliefs and what it means to be a Jew, go to:
www.waylinks.co.uk/series/religiontoday/Judaism

➤ The Ten Commandments on the wall of a synagogue in Safed, Israel. They remind every worshipper of the importance of these laws. They are written in Hebrew.

'Teaching'

The word *Torah* means 'teaching'. The Torah is at the heart of Jewish life and worship. It contains stories about the early history of the Jewish people, commandments, rules, poems and sayings about life.

Every week, all year round, a part of the Torah is read in the synagogue. Studying the Torah is a very important part of Jewish life. The role of the rabbi is to teach the Torah. For Jews it is the source of holiness and eternal life.

▼ *The scrolls of the Torah are kept in the Ark – a cupboard at the front of every synagogue.*

The giving of the Torah

A Jewish legend tells how, when the Torah was given to the people by God on Mount Sinai, the mountain burst into flower, the birds stopped singing and the whole universe became quiet and still – as if waiting for something very beautiful to happen. This was followed by thunder, lightning and a thick cloud which covered the whole mountain. God came down on to the mountain in fire and the whole place shook.

▲ *The scrolls of the Torah are written out by hand by a specially trained* **scribe**.

The Messiah

Messiah means 'the **anointed** one'. In ancient times, kings were anointed with oil when they were crowned. The Messiah is a king. Orthodox Jews are waiting for this king, who will put everything right on earth. Progressive Jews look for an age of love and peace. Many Jews pray each day for the Messiah to come.

The afterlife

Jewish Scriptures say that there is a life after death. They teach that when a person dies their soul survives in *Sheol*, a place of darkness and shadows. God will reward those who have lived a righteous life and punish sinners. When the Messiah comes, then the righteous will be brought back to life.

21

Jewish holy books

The Jewish Bible, or **Tenakh**, is the holy book for all Jews. The Tenakh is a very old collection of writings. It has three parts: the Torah (teachings), the Prophets (*Nevi'im*), and the Writings (*Ketuvim*; songs and sayings). The parts are divided into different sections, called books. There are 39 books in the Jewish Bible.

The Jewish Bible contains many different kinds of writing. It tells the history of the Jews from the creation of the world to the time when they were exiled from Israel. There are many songs, poems and wise sayings. The Jewish Bible tells how God loved and guided the Jews. There are also laws and rules which Jews try to follow.

▼ *A scroll of the Torah is read in a synagogue in Havana, Cuba. Reading from the Torah is a great honour.*

◄ *This stained glass window in a synagogue in the UK celebrates the festival of Simchat Torah.*

weblinks

For more information about the Jewish Scriptures, go to: www.waylinks.co.uk/series/ religiontoday/Judaism

Simchat Torah

The Jews value the first part of their Bible – the Torah – very highly. The festival of *Simchat Torah* is when Jews thank God for giving them the Torah. During the year the whole of the Torah, from start to finish, is read in the synagogue on the Sabbath day. On Simchat Torah, the last part of the last book is read. The reading then starts again with the first chapter of the first book, Genesis. There is no break between the two readings. This shows that God's word is eternal, without beginning or end.

In our own words

"*As a Jew the Torah means a lot to me. The commandments in the Torah are my everyday guide to living. The characters in the Torah, especially Abraham and Moses, are just like real people with many faults and their good points as well. I do not think that the Torah is too hard to follow. It tells me how I should treat other people as if they really matter. I want to live the way it teaches me to.*"

Rachel, aged 14, UK

The Prophets and the Writings

The Prophets and Writings are also important parts of the Tenakh.

The Prophets

A prophet is a person who has been chosen by God to act as his messenger. It is someone who speaks on God's behalf to his people.

The books of the Jewish Scriptures that tell the story of the prophets are named after them. The books named after the prophets Isaiah, Jeremiah and Ezekiel are long and important. There are also twelve books named after less important prophets, such as Hosea, Obadiah, Jonah and Malachi.

◄ A drawing of the prophet Isaiah by the 19th-century French artist Gustav Doré. This picture is in the Tel Aviv Museum in Israel.

The Writings

The Writings are a collection of poems, songs and wise sayings which make up the final part of the Tenakh. The most popular of these writings is the Book of Psalms, a collection of 150 songs. King David and his son, Solomon, are thought to have written many of them. Another part of the Writings is the Book of Proverbs, which has many wise sayings.

From the Psalms

'Oh praise the Lord. Praise God in his holiness. Praise him in the firmament of his power.
Praise him in his mighty acts. Praise him according to his excellent greatness.
Praise him with the sound of the trumpet; praise him upon the lute and harp.'
(Psalm 150:1-3)

'The Lord is my shepherd, I shall not be in want.
He makes me lie down in green pastures
He leads me beside still waters,
He restores my soul.'
(Psalm 23:1-3)

▲ King Solomon and the Queen of Sheba are pictured on this Jewish rug, made in Kashan, Iran. Solomon became famous for his great wisdom. It is said that he wrote three books of the Jewish Bible – Ecclesiastes, the Book of Proverbs and the Song of Solomon.

3 Jewish life and worship

Jews do not have to go to the synagogue to worship God. The way they live their everyday lives is also their way of worshipping God. Jews believe that you can praise God even when doing everyday things such as eating a meal or going to bed.

The mezuzah

The *mezuzah* is a tiny scroll. Written on it are the first two paragraphs of the Shema (see page 19). Mezuzah scrolls are placed inside small wooden or plastic casings and attached to the right-hand doorposts of every room in the house – apart from the bathroom and toilet. A mezuzah is also put next to the front door. When traditional Jews come home or go out, they touch the mezuzah and kiss their fingers. This reminds them of the promise in the Torah: 'You are blessed when you come in and blessed when you go out.'

➤ *A mezuzah attached to the doorpost of a Jewish home.*

Kosher food

The word kosher means something that is 'allowed'. Religious Jews eat only kosher food. The Torah explains what Jews cannot eat:

• Certain animals such as pigs, camels and hares. But chicken, duck and turkey are allowed. Jews only eat seafood that has fins and scales

• Animals have to be killed for food in a way that drains all the blood from their bodies

• Meat and milky foods must not be eaten together

In our own words

"I don't really understand all of the kosher rules. When I asked the rabbi at my synagogue to explain them to me, he said that in the old days there were two reasons for these rules. The first was to make sure no one got sick when our ancestors were travelling across the desert. The second reason is that by following these rules we show obedience to God. We may not understand everything that God tells us to do, but that is when we have to trust him the most."

Anna, aged 15, USA

weblinks

For more information about kosher food, go to:
www.waylinks.co.uk/series/religiontoday/Judaism

The KOSHER Store

TURKEY BREAST	4.59lb	CORNED BEEF	6.69lb	RO
SMOKED CURED TURKEY BREAST	4.99lb	FRENCH PASTRAMI	7.99lb	SAL
TURKEY PASTRAMI	4.39lb	HARD BEEF SALAMI	4.99lb	BOL

◄ A kosher butcher in a department store in Austin, Texas, USA. Every kosher butcher's shop is examined by Jewish religious leaders and given a certificate that says its meat is kosher.

The Sabbath

Shabbat, the Sabbath day, is the Jewish holy day of rest. It reminds Jews of two things: that after creating the world in six days, God rested on the seventh day, and that God saved the Israelites from slavery in Egypt (see page 12).

The Sabbath day

The Jewish Sabbath begins on Friday evening and finishes at sunset on Saturday evening. On Friday, before Sabbath begins, the house is cleaned and tidied and a special meal is prepared. The meal is an important family and religious occasion.

weblinks

For more information about the Sabbath day go to:
www.waylinks.co.uk/series/religiontoday/Judaism

For many Jewish families the Sabbath day begins when the mother of the house lights two or more candles and says a prayer to welcome the holy day. Traditionally, the father and older children start the Sabbath day in the synagogue. Everyone comes home for the meal, and a parent blesses his or her children.

➤ A Jewish mother and her daughter light the candles that mark the beginning of the Sabbath day. When the male members of the family come home from the synagogue, the family eat together.

The Sabbath day ends with a special ceremony called *Havdalah*. Blessings are given over wine, spices and a plaited candle, and everyone exchanges wishes for a good and 'sweet' week ahead.

Sabbath day rules

Many activities are forbidden for Orthodox Jews on the Sabbath day. They include lighting a fire, cooking, switching on any electrical equipment, playing a musical instrument, driving a car, using public transport such as a bus, train or aeroplane, writing, watching television and riding a bicycle or motorcycle.

◀ *This silver holder contains spices such as cinnamon, cloves, nutmeg and bay leaves. It is used during the Havdalah ceremony which marks the end of the Sabbath day.*

Worship in the synagogue

Synagogue means a place for 'meeting together'. In traditional synagogues, there must be at least ten men present for certain parts of the service. In Progressive synagogues, women are counted in the total.

Special clothes

Many traditional Jewish men wear a skullcap (*kippah*) all of the time, both inside and outside the synagogue. For morning prayers, many Jews wear a special prayer shawl, called a *tallit*, over their clothes. The tallit has tassels to help worshippers remember the many commandments in the Torah.

During weekday services at home or in the synagogue, religious Jews wear two small leather boxes called *tefillin*, which are tied with leather straps in the middle of the forehead and on the left arm. These boxes contain words from the Jewish Bible, reminding each worshipper that the word of God should be in their mind and heart.

The words inside a tefillin can be written only by trained scribes. Once in a while, the boxes are opened by an expert and checked. If the scroll is damaged, then it must be replaced.

▼ *Tallits hang in a row. Many Jewish men are buried with their tallits.*

The rabbi

A rabbi is a person who is well-respected in the Jewish community because he or she is highly trained in the Torah as well as in Jewish law and tradition. In Orthodox synagogues a rabbi is always male, but in other Jewish groups, rabbis can be male or female. During Sabbath worship, the rabbi leads the people in prayer, reads from the Torah and gives a sermon. He or she also conducts weddings, funerals and religious classes. They also visit sick people and homes where someone has died.

Three rabbis form a Bet Din. This is a court of Jewish law. This court gives permission for marriages, settles arguments and interprets Jewish law. It also plays an important part in granting divorces, called gets, to Jewish couples. The get is a 'religious' divorce which means that they can remarry in a synagogue.

▼ The rabbi is an important part of a Jewish community. Here Rabbi Yaakov Rapoport and his helpers knead and roll matzoh in Dewitt, USA. The matzoh, a type of flat bread, is an important food during the festival of Passover.

Jewish festivals

There are many Jewish festivals. The most important are *Rosh Hashanah*, *Yom Kippur*, Sukkot, Shavuot, *Hanukkah*, Purim and Passover.

Rosh Hashanah

Rosh Hashanah is the Jewish New Year. It begins the Ten Days of **Penitence** which end with Yom Kippur (the Day of **Atonement**). It is a time for Jews to think about the past year, and to try to right any wrongs they may have done. During Rosh Hashanah a ram's horn, called a *shofar*, is blown one hundred times in the synagogue. The sound of the shofar reminds Jews of a person crying and calls them together.

Yom Kippur

Yom Kippur is a day of prayer and **fasting**. On this day Jews follow the example of the angels who, tradition says, do not eat or drink. At this time Jews ask God's forgiveness. They also think of how to live a better life for God and with others.

▼ *A rabbi blows a shofar. The sound of a shofar symbolizes sorrow.*

➤ *A booth built for the festival of Sukkot in Jerusalem. This is a public booth, but many people make their own booths to celebrate this festival.*

━━━ weblinks↖ ━━━

To find out the dates of the main Jewish festivals for the coming year, go to:
www.waylinks.co.uk/series/religiontoday/Judaism

Sukkot

Sukkot is a very happy Jewish festival. Many families build a booth in their garden. This booth is a hut decorated with flowers and fruit, with a roof made of leaves and branches. Many families eat their meals in the booth, and some even sleep in it. The booth is a symbol of trust in God, who protected the Israelites during forty years of travelling in the wilderness (see page 12).

Shavuot

Shavuot celebrates when God gave the Torah to Moses. Jews decorate their synagogues with lots of flowers to remind worshippers of how Mount Sinai burst into flower when God gave Moses the Torah (see page 20).

In our own words

"I love Sukkot because I enjoy building a booth in the garden with my parents, brother and sister. The most important festival, though, is Pesach because it is the festival of freedom. We remember that God brought all of our ancestors out of Egypt – the place of slavery. We need to remember that we are descended from slaves. This makes us appreciate our freedom. Then there is seder night (see page 35). This is a big family gathering."

Amroth, aged 16, Israel

Hanukkah

This festival is also known as the Festival of Light. It celebrates the victory of a Jewish family called the Maccabees over the Syrian army in the 2nd century BCE. The king's soldiers had damaged the Temple. When the Temple was repaired, the Jews decided to hold a ceremony. They needed to light the lamp that burns in front of the Ark – but they only had enough oil for one night. Miraculously, it lasted for eight days – enough time for new oil to be prepared. Hanukkah reminds Jews of the restoration of the temple and the miracle of the oil. Each day of Hanukkah a candle is lit on a special candlestick with eight branches.

Purim

Purim celebrates the story of Esther who saved the Jewish people about 2,500 years ago. This is an exciting festival for children. The story of Esther is read out in the synagogue and children dress up in the costumes of the characters. Every time the name Haman (the villain in the story) is mentioned, the children make as much noise as possible using whistles, rattles and dustbin lids – or by just stamping their feet!

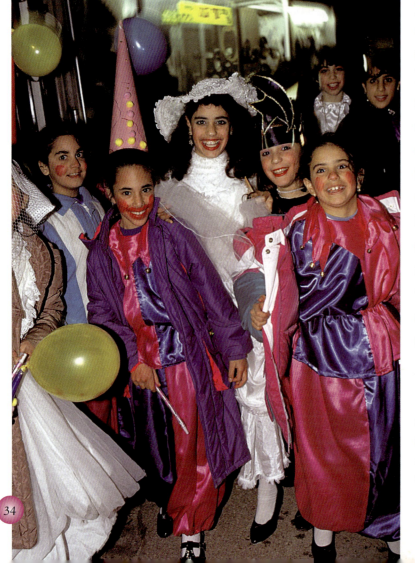

◄ Children in Jerusalem dressed up for the festival of Purim. The costumes represent characters from the story of Esther.

Passover

Passover (Pesach) is an important Jewish festival. Passover remembers how God rescued the Israelites from slavery in Egypt. It is called 'Passover' because the Angel of Death passed over the houses of the Jews and punished the Egyptians.

Seder

During Passover, Jews eat a special meal, called *seder*. Jews also eat a special flat bread at this time to remind them that when the Israelites left Egypt, they did not have time to take yeast with them to make their bread rise.

▼ *A seder plate. While the food is eaten, Jews remember the story of their slavery and escape from Egypt*

The seder plate

The seder plate on the table holds a number of different foods to remind everyone of the meaning of Passover. Two of them, a roasted egg and a roasted lamb bone, represent worship in the old Temple, but they are not eaten. Bitter herbs are eaten, a reminder of the bitter lives of the slaves; one or two green vegetables to remind everyone that this is a Spring festival; and a mixture of chopped apple, nuts, cinnamon and wine to symbolize the cement used by the Israelite slaves when they were building houses for their Egyptian masters.

Being Jewish

Being Jewish affects a person's whole life. There are Jewish ceremonies or rituals to mark all of the important times in a Jew's life.

Circumcision

Circumcision is the oldest Jewish religious practice that is still carried out today. It goes all the way back to Abraham. Abraham was told by God to circumcise all the male members of his family. It has always been carried out on the eighth day after a boy's birth. The ceremony must take place on that day even if it falls on the Sabbath. Only illness is allowed to delay it.

▼ *A Jewish baby boy is circumcised. The operation is performed by a trained person called a mohel.*

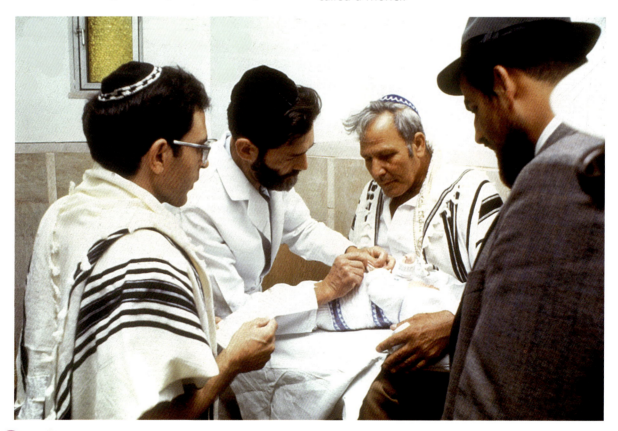

Bar Mitzvah

Bar Mitzvah marks a boy's entry into adulthood. It is held on the first Sabbath day after a boy's thirteenth birthday. Until a boy's Bar Mitzvah, his father has been responsible for his son's spiritual education. Now this responsibility is passed to the boy himself.

Girls join adult Jewish society a year earlier than boys. In many synagogues girls have a *Bat Mitzvah*, when they read from the Torah. In many Orthodox synagogues, girls might give a talk about the Bible reading for that week.

In our own words

"I have just celebrated my Bar Mitzvah. I learned Hebrew in our classes at the synagogue – it is frightening to stand up in front of all your relations and friends to read from the Torah! But I'd practised it a lot, and it went well. The service was followed by a special meal where everyone gave me presents – that was very nice! I stood up to thank them for their love and kindness as well as telling them my hopes for a Jewish future."

Joseph, 13, UK

◄ A Bar/Bat Mitzvah class is held for both boys and girls in a Conservative synagogue in Tel Aviv, Israel. In this class, children are taught biblical Hebrew as well as more about their Jewish faith.

Marriage

Judaism encourages Jews to marry someone who is also Jewish.

During the wedding service the bride and groom stand under a *chuppah* (canopy), which is sometimes decorated with flowers. This canopy is a symbol of the home that the couple are going to set up. The couple drink wine together as the wedding blessings are spoken. Then the groom gives the bride a ring and formally takes her in marriage. The *ketubah*, the marriage certificate, is read aloud and signed, before the groom crushes a glass beneath his feet. This reminds Jews of the destruction of the Temple.

▼ A Jewish couple stand beneath a chuppah at their wedding. A Jewish wedding can take place out of doors, in the synagogue or in the home.

Death

Jewish tradition says that a Jewish funeral and burial must take place as soon as possible after death – ideally within 24 hours. Funeral services must be simple, with the body being placed in a basic coffin. This is because Jews believe that everyone, rich and poor, is equal in death. Orthodox Jews do not allow **cremation**, although it is permitted by Progressive Jews.

For almost a year, close relatives recite the *kaddish*, a special prayer, every day. A special candle is lit each year on the anniversary of the person's death.

From the Kaddish

This prayer praises God who is the giver of all life.

'Let us magnify and let us sanctify the great name of God in the world which he created according to his will. May his kingdom come in your lifetime, and in your days, and in the lifetime of the family of Israel – quickly and speedily may it come... He is far beyond any blessing or song, any honour or any consolation that can be spoken of in this world.'

▼ *A girl lights a memorial candle at the grave of Jewish Prime Minister, Yitzak Rabin.*

# 5 Judaism in today's world

Judaism is a very old religion. But like other religions, it needs to be able to face modern problems. Jews try to see how the Torah can be applied today.

Justice for everyone

Jews believe that the Torah contains everything that Jews need to know about how they should behave and what is expected of them by God. Over the centuries, rabbis have drawn up a list of laws from the Torah, called the *Halakhah*. Jews believe that these laws can bring justice for everyone.

Jews believe that if everyone listened to the Torah, which says 'love your neighbour as you love yourself' (Leviticus 19:18), then everything would be well in the world. The Torah says that those who break God's laws must be held responsible for their actions.

The Torah says that if someone takes another life, they should give up their own. However, the state of Israel abolished the death penalty for almost all crimes in the 1950s.

Remembering the Holocaust

When the Second World War ended in 1945, the horror of the Holocaust was revealed to the world. People were deeply shocked. Many people of all faiths feel strongly that everything possible must be done to make sure that these events are never forgotten and never repeated. Today

Choosing judges

This is what is expected of judges in the Torah:

'Appoint judges and officials for each of your tribes in every town the Lord your God is giving you, and they shall judge the people fairly... Do not accept a bribe, for a bribe blinds the eyes of the wise and twists the words of the righteous. Follow justice and justice alone, so that you may live and possess the land the Lord your God is giving you.'

(Deuteronomy 16:18-20)

Jews and non-Jews all over the world are involved in many projects on the Holocaust, including interviewing survivors and trying to get money and possessions back that were stolen from Jews.

A special museum

Berlin, in Germany, was the capital of the **Nazi** party which persecuted Jews before and during the Second World War, so the new Jewish Museum there is particularly important.

The Jewish Museum in Berlin was designed by the Polish architect Daniel Libeskind and opened in 2001. The building is in the shape of a long zigzag, partly based on the idea of an opened Star of David.

The Jewish Museum celebrates the achievements of German Jews, as well as remembering the Holocaust and the millions who died.

▼ The modern design of the Jewish Museum in Berlin.

Prejudice against Jews

For centuries Jews have been the victims of prejudice. Jews have often found themselves to be the butt of jokes about their religious traditions, beliefs, ways of worshipping and clothing. In the worst cases, Jewish graves, kosher shops and synagogues have been vandalised and attacked.

Racism

Prejudice is not something that happens only to Jews. Many groups of people are picked on because they are in some way 'different'. At its worst, prejudice can grow into hatred and violence. When people hate a whole race, it is called 'racism'.

Welcoming foreigners

The Torah says:

'When an alien [foreigner] lives with you in your land, do not ill-treat him. The alien living with you must be treated as one of your native-born. Love him as yourself, for you were aliens in Egypt.

(Leviticus 19:33-34)

Jews believe that racism is wrong because all people were created by God and so are valued by God. In the book of Genesis, the Torah says: 'God created human beings, making them to be like himself'.

Jews believe that if people are made by God, and are like God, it is wrong to hate them. Jews strongly believe that it is wrong to mistreat anyone just because they are different.

◄ *Jewish prisoners in Dachau concentration camp in Germany cheer American soldiers at the end of the Second World War, in 1945.*

In our own words

"I am a Jew. Other people know that I am a Jew and they accept me for what I am. That goes for all my friends. I have not suffered from prejudice but I do know people who have."

Rebecca, aged 17, USA

▼ A woman looks at Jewish graves damaged at a cemetery in St Petersburg, Russia, in 2004. In this attack, the gravestones were painted with the symbol used by the Nazis during the Second World War.

The rich and the poor

Judaism teaches that everyone has a duty to help the poor, since no-one chooses to be poor. At festival times, money should be given so that the poor can join in the celebrations.

Jewish Scriptures give practical advice on helping the poor. They say that at harvest time, farmers should leave corn growing at the edges of their fields for the poor to collect.

Tzedaka

The teaching of the Jewish Scriptures is that everyone should give ten per cent of their income to the poor. It is like a tax and it is called *tzedaka*. Even someone who has received charity because they are poor is expected to give part of what they have away to other poor people. The word tzedaka means 'justice', and giving charity is considered a fair and right thing to do.

The poor in Jewish Scriptures

'There will always be poor people in the land. Therefore I command you to be open-handed towards your brothers and towards the poor and needy in your land.' (Deuteronomy 15:11)

'When God gives any man wealth and possessions and enables him to enjoy them, to accept his lot and be happy in his work – this is a gift of God.' (Ecclesiastes 5:19)

'Naked a man comes from his mother's womb, and as he comes, so he departs. He takes nothing from his labour that he can carry in his hand.' (Ecclesiastes 5:15)

▼ Jewish charity boxes. The money collected was once used to buy land in Israel but is now mostly used to provide clean drinking water for that country.

Israel and anti-semitism

The continuing violence between Palestinians and Israelis in Israel affects Jews outside of that country. People who disagree with the political decisions of the Israeli government may use this as an excuse to dislike Jews, wherever they live. Many organisations have been set up so that people of different faiths can meet together and understand each other better.

'Operation Solomon'

For centuries a community of up to 500,000 Jews lived in northern Ethiopia, isolated from the rest of the Jewish world. This community called itself Beta Israel – the 'house of Israel'. In the 19th century, Beta Israel started to make links with the worldwide community of Jews. In the 1970s, these Ethiopian Jews started to suffer from prejudice, and many wanted to move to Israel, but the Ethiopian government stopped them. Terrible famines in the 1980s led Israel to mount many rescue operations for Ethiopian Jews. In 1984 and 1985 almost 8,000 Jews were rescued and brought to Israel. In the following five years, more Jews were taken from Ethiopia. Then, in 1991, a secret Israeli airlift rescued over 14,000 Jews from Ethiopia. This was known as 'Operation Solomon'. There are now 36,000 Ethiopian Jews living in Israel.

➤ *An Israeli leads a group of Ethiopian Jews to a waiting plane at Addis Ababa airport in May 1991, during 'Operation Solomon'.*

Glossary

adultery When a married person is unfaithful to their partner with someone else.

anointed To apply oil to someone in a ceremony.

Ark The cupboard in a synagogue in which the Torah is kept.

Assyrian An early civilization to the east of Israel, which at its height covered the whole of the western part of the Middle East, including present-day Iraq, Israel, Jordan, Syria and Egypt.

Atonement Making amends for wrongs we have committed.

Babylonian An early civilization to the east of Israel, based in present-day Iraq.

circumcision A medical operation where a boy's foreskin is removed.

concentration camp A kind of camp where prisoners are forced to do hard work for little food. During the Second World War, many Jews were killed as soon as they arrived in German concentration camps.

convert To persuade someone to change their religion.

cremation When dead bodies are burnt until only ash is left.

exile Being sent away from the country where you were born or where you live.

famine When there is not enough food in a place and people go hungry.

fasting Not eating.

Holocaust Hitler's plan to kill all the Jews in the world, which was put into action during the Second World War. Six million Jews were killed.

idol A statue or painting that is worshipped as a god.

Inquisition A Christian religious court that often condemned non-believers to torture or death.

Israelites An early name for Jews. Jews in the Bible are called Israelites.

Nazi The political party that took over Germany during the Second World War, headed by Adolf Hitler.

Orthodox The most traditional branch of Judaism. Orthodox religions follow their holy books to the letter without changing their meaning.

Ottoman Empire A Turkish Muslim empire that lasted over 600 years, from 1299 to 1922. It included all of the Middle East except Iran and the desert of Arabia.

penitence Showing that we feel bad for something we have done wrong.

persecute To treat someone very badly.

plague A disaster.

Progressive A modern branch of Judaism which believes Judaism should change with the times.

prophet Someone who brings messages from God.

rabbi A special teacher and leader of Judaism.

Sabbath The Jewish holy day of rest.

scribe A person who writes documents for other people for payment.

Scriptures Religious writings.

secular Not religious.

Shema ('hear') The Jewish name for the words of Deuteronomy 6:4. The Shema is recited twice each day by Jews as a statement of their faith in God.

synagogue The Jewish meeting place for prayer, study and teaching.

Temple The Jewish Temple in Jerusalem was first built by Solomon around 950BCE and destroyed by the Babylonians in 586BCE.

Tenakh The name given to the Jewish Scriptures made up of the Torah, the Prophets and the Writings.

Torah Jews use this word to mean two different things. It can mean the first five books of the Jewish Scriptures. It is also used to mean 'teaching'.

Timeline

BCE

2000-1900	Time of Abraham, Isaac and Jacob
1600s	Israelites are slaves in Egypt
1200s-1100s	Moses leads the Israelites out of slavery and receives the Torah and the Ten Commandments. The Israelites conquer Canaan.
c.1000	King David unites the tribes in Jerusalem
c.960	Solomon succeeds David and builds the first Temple
c.920	Solomon dies and his kingdom divides into Israel in the north and Judah in the south
722	Israel conquered by the Assyrians
586	Judah falls to the Babylonians. Temple in Jerusalem destroyed and Jewish population deported.
167	Judas Maccabeous leads a revolt against the Greeks
63	Romans conquer Palestine. Jewish communities spread throughout Roman Empire.
40-4	Romans put Herod the Great on the throne of Judea

CE

66-70	Jews revolt against the Romans. Romans destroy the Temple built by Herod the Great in Jerusalem
638	Muslims conquer Jerusalem
1066	Jews settle in England
1290	Jews thrown out of England
1306	Jews thrown out of parts of France
1348	The Black Death: Jews are blamed and massacred throughout Europe
1492	Spanish Jews given choice of conversion to Christianity or to leave Spain
1497	Jews thrown out of Portugal
1881-2	Jews persecuted in Russia
1939-45	Second World War: six million Jews killed in Holocaust
1948	Founding of the State of Israel
1967	The 'Six-Day War' between Israel and Egypt, Syria and Jordan
1979	Peace treaty between Israel and Egypt

Further reading

World Religions: Judaism by Angela Wood (Franklin Watts, 1999)

Religions of the World: Judaism by Sue Penney (Heinemann, 2003)

Prayer and Worship: Jewish by Anita Ganeri (Franklin Watts, 2006)

Let's Find Out About Jewish Synagogues by Mandy Ross (Raintree, 2006)

Index